One Body

*Just as each of us has one
body with many members,
and these members do not
all have the same function,
so in Christ we who are many
form one body, and each
member belongs to all
the others.*
Romans 12:4–5

Connected

Read Romans 12:3–8.

*We who are many form one body, and
each member belongs
to all the others.*
Romans 12:5

Of all the examples our Lord could have used to describe
our relationship with him and each other, he chose the
human body. Such an intimate picture of harmony!

The body is a single unit. No part is a separate entity. Your
hands and feet and face are each a part of you. They belong
to you. They are not independent of you. That's how closely
God has connected us to the rest of his Church and to
himself.

Colossians 1:17–20 describes how Christ himself fits into
this picture:

He is before all things, and in him all things hold together.
And he is the head of the body, the church; he is the beginning
and the firstborn from among the dead, so that in
everything he might have the supremacy.

For God was pleased to have all his fullness dwell in him,
and through him to reconcile to himself all things,
whether things on earth or things in heaven,
by making peace through his blood, shed on the cross.

4

Thank You
for
Serving the Savior

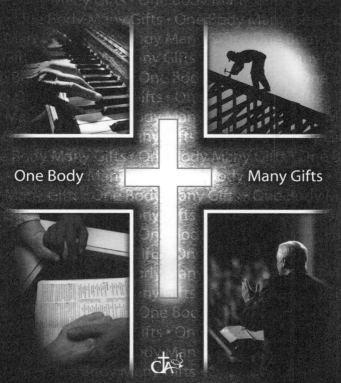

One Body   Many Gifts

So we, being many, are one body in Christ.
Romans 12:5 KJV

Carol Albrecht • Jessica Bordeleau • Pat Mitchell • Tim Wesemann

The mission of CTA is
to glorify God by providing purposeful
products that lift up and encourage
the body of Christ—
because we love him.

www.CTAinc.com

Thank You for Serving the Savior

Carol Albrecht (Week 2)
Jessica Bordeleau (Week 1)
Pat Mitchell (Week 3)
Tim Wesemann (Weeks 4 & 5)

Copyright © 2011 CTA, Inc.
1625 Larkin Williams Rd.
Fenton, MO 63026

Unless otherwise indicated, Scripture is taken from the Holy Bible, New International Version®, NIV®. Copyright © 1973, 1978, 1984 by Biblica, Inc.™ Used by permission of Zondervan. All rights reserved worldwide. www.zondervan.com

Scripture quotations marked ESV are from The Holy Bible, English Standard Version® (ESV®), copyright © 2001 by Crossway, a publishing ministry of Good News Publishers. Used by permission. All rights reserved.

Scripture quotations marked KJV are from the King James Version of the Bible.

Scripture quotation so indicated is taken from The Message. Copyright © 1993, 1994, 1995, 1996, 2000, 2001, 2002. Used by permission of NavPress Publishing Group.

ISBN 978-1-935404-21-7
Printed in Thailand

hrist is the head of the body. He does the planning. He
irects the rest of the body as it acts and moves. He oversees
he care and provision given to each of the other parts.

n the human body, the head isn't a distant and remote force
hat merely observes, leaving the body to fend for itself. No!
he head is intimately connected to the body and concerned
bout it. In the same way, our Lord Jesus is intimately
onnected to and concerned about us.

ur Savior demonstrated that concern by dying for us. That is
he length to which he will go to have a relationship with us.
y faith, Jesus' holiness is applied to us, and it makes us part of
is very own Body, his family, the community of the faithful. He
ecame one of us to make us one with each other in him!

We are connected to Christ not as
slaves to a master, but as feet and
hands to the head of a body. God's
love for us is extravagant,
amazing, and intimate! Jesus
didn't stay in his tomb, and
neither will we! We will follow our
head into eternal life,
harmoniously connected to each
other and to our Lord forever!

**Lord Jesus, thank you for
making me your own and for
giving me a place in your Body!
Show me . . .**

Serving Single-Handedly?

Read Numbers 11:4–17.

*They will help you carry the burden
of the people so that you will
not have to carry it alone.*
Numbers 11:17

"I can't do it anymore! These people are driving me crazy! How am I suppose to love and care for people that act like this?!" Sometimes serving God's people seems like an impossible task.

In Numbers 11, Moses has a classic church-worker meltdown. Overwhelmed at the people's complaints and demands, he brings his frustration to the Lord (vv. 11–12):

*[Moses] asked the LORD, "Why have you brought this trouble on
your servant? What have I done to displease you that you put
the burden of all these people on me? Did I conceive all
these people? Did I give them birth? Why do you
tell me to carry them ...?"*

Sound familiar? It comforts me to know that the great prophet Moses, the servant who spoke directly with God and witnessed such incredible miracles, had days of stress and distress, just like we do. Caring for God's people is a lot of work. It's rarely easy. Sometimes we get so busy caring and helping others that we fail to let others help and care for us.

od's response to Moses' prayer is telling:

> *Bring me seventy of Israel's elders who are known to you as leaders and officials among the people .... I will take of the Spirit that is on you and put the Spirit on them. They will help you carry the burden of the people so that you will not have to carry it alone.*
> Numbers 11:16–17

od didn't require Moses to carry the burden all alone. He pened Moses' eyes to others in the Body of believers who ould help, and he showed Moses how to allow others to hare the burden. God doesn't require you to serve alone ither. He has connected you to others who can support you, erving alongside you. Do you let them?

wasn't until I faced a set of overwhelming tasks in my youth rogramming that I finally found myself recruiting a team of olunteers. It meant giving up some control, but I gained so uch more joy!

we insist on serving alone, whether from pride or from erfectionism or from some other sin, we deny others the lessings of serving. We deny ourselves the comfort of seeing esus at work through his Body. How thankful we can be that esus died for all our sins—even those we commit as we serve im! And how thankful we can be that he hasn't left us alone. hank him today for those who surround you, who serve as his ands to comfort and relieve you.

ord Jesus, forgive me for my failures to ask for help and upport. Send just the right people to . . .

Service Essentials

Read Luke 10:38–42.

You are worried and upset about many things, but only one thing is needed.
Luke 10:41–42

The last time you were on a plane, you probably heard an announcement like this: "If oxygen levels in the cabin become too low, air masks will drop down from the overhead compartment. Attach your own mask first; then assist others ..."

Selfish? Not at all! If you try to help others before you have enough oxygen yourself, your help won't last long. You'll be unconscious. Then, dead!

Our relationship with our Savior is something like that flow of oxygen. We stay spiritually alive as we are connected to him through his Word. Again and again, we read of his great love shown to us in the forgiveness of our sins and in the other countless blessings that flow to us from Calvary's cross.

At one point I realized I was encouraging others to be in the Word—and that all my personal time with Jesus had faded away in the busyness of my ministry. You, too?

We're not alone. Luke 10 describes another such servant, a friend of the Savior (vv. 38–40 ESV):

Thank You for Serving the Savior

Now as they went on their way, Jesus entered a village. And a woman named Martha welcomed him into her house. And she had a sister called Mary, who sat at the Lord's feet and listened to his teaching. But Martha was distracted with much serving.

Traditionally, we've been taught that meal preparations distracted Martha. Recently, though, scholars have noted the word *serving* often referred to things like caring for the sick, praying with the dying, and other people-oriented activities.

If so, it's easier to understand why Martha saw her sister's choice as lazy and selfish. No wonder she raised the issue with the Lord. Yet, how his answer surprises us! Mary is doing something important, too—better, in fact!

Think about your own devotional practices. What good things most often push the best thing off your calendar? What gets in the way of your time in the Word and prayer?

Ever gentle, Jesus reaches out to bring the gift of repentance into our lives. He assures us of his pardon and ongoing love. And he reminds us of his priorities for our lives. Time with him day by day improves our service and makes it possible. It isn't selfish or greedy. It's essential!

Lord Jesus, thank you for your forgiveness! Assure me of it, and teach me to recalibrate my priorities . . .

Appendix People

Read Luke 19:1–10.

All the people saw this and began to mutter, "He has gone to be the guest of a 'sinner.'"
Luke 19:7

We each have unique gifts and talents. We each play a part in the Body of Christ. It all makes sense in a Sunday-school-lesson kind of way, until we get to "appendix people." You know them—people who are difficult to love, hard to work with, and uncomfortable to be around. We think of them as disposable. We'd rather cut them out than deal with them.

While we take comfort in being part of the Body of believers ourselves, we grow uncomfortable when we remember the "appendix people" belong, too. Jesus loves difficult people. That's good to remember, because you and I sometimes fall into that "difficult" category ourselves!

Over and over in the Gospels we see Jesus standing up for the kinds of people we'd rather not interact with. As we read the Scriptures, we may whitewash the tax collectors and prostitutes our Lord befriended. They must have been devout, simply misunderstood by others. Right?

But what if they were the obnoxious, annoying, self-centered, hard-to-deal-with types that drive us crazy in our own ministries even today?

Consider the tax collector Zacchaeus. Jesus did more than tolerate Zacchaeus. The Lord sought him out and befriended him! He demonstrated in a dramatic way the fact that all the parts of his Body are connected. All belong—even the ones we consider expendable. No one lives outside the boundaries of Jesus' self-sacrificing care and concern. That kind of love changes everything. It changed Zacchaeus (v. 8):

> [He] stood up and said to the Lord, "Look, Lord! Here and now I give half of my possessions to the poor, and if I have cheated anybody out of anything, I will pay back four times the amount."

In response, Jesus noted (vv. 9–10):

> Today salvation has come to this house, because this man, too, is a son of Abraham. For the Son of Man came to seek and to save what was lost.

Once lost, we have now been found—and claimed—by our Savior. This makes it possible to love and accept one another.

By the way, *Science Daily* recently reported that the human appendix stores healthy bacteria for the body's use. It seems that all our parts have a purpose, even the appendix!

Dear Jesus, forgive my loveless attitudes. Teach me to love as you have loved me, difficult as I often am . . .

Alone?

Read John 17:20–26.

My prayer is not for them alone. I pray also for those who will believe in me through their message.
John 17:20

The stay-at-home parent who hasn't had a real conversation in days. The church worker buried under piles of papers and to-do lists who sits in an empty church all week. The businessperson surrounded by cubicles inhabited by denizens who type quietly at computer keyboards all day long. Opportunities for loneliness abound in our culture. We can feel alone even in a crowd.

Those of us who volunteer in churches and those who serve on the professional staff, too, can find the experience of ministry isolating. The weight of caring for others can leave us feeling we're alone with their burdens. This can turn into anxiety and stress. We may swim alone in a sea of worry.

Our Lord knows all about the isolation of ministry. Jesus himself experienced it. He reminds us again and again in his Word that we are not alone, that we are part of his Body, the community of believers, connected to each other in him.

In John 17:20–22 we read the words Jesus prayed the night before he died. He prayed these words for us—for you and me:

My prayer is not for them alone. I pray also for those who will believe in me through their message, that all of them may be one, Father, just as you are in me and I am in you. May they also be in us so that the world may believe that you have sent me. I have given them the glory that you gave me, that they may be one as we are one.

In this prayer Jesus asks the Father to make us (the Church on earth) one. He prayed that you would be connected to others, just as he is connected to the Father. We are not alone. We are part of Christ's Body, a community of believers with something in common: our Savior Jesus Christ, himself!

That common bond can transcend our isolation and worry. Our relationships with each other reflect our connection to our Lord. He cares for us through others! By sending his Son to live and die for you, our heavenly Father made it possible for you to live in him and with him both now and forever! You are not alone!

Lord Jesus, you prayed for me and pray for me still. You know the concerns of my heart. Teach me to give those concerns to you, especially today . . .

For Reflection . . .

Belonging is such a beautiful word. A warm, happy word. We long for the acceptance of belonging.

But belonging carries with it responsibilities. When we belong to the church, for example, we're expected to care for and support other members. That's especially true in the Church where we are "all one in Christ Jesus" (Galatians 3:28).

Those three little words, *in Christ Jesus*, make all the difference. God has chosen us! Not for anything we've done for him, but because of what Jesus did for us on Calvary's cross.

You are forgiven! You belong in the Body of Christ! What difference will that make this week?

One Heart

I appeal to you, brothers, in the name of our Lord Jesus Christ, that all of you agree with one another so that there may be no divisions among you and that you may be perfectly united in mind and thought.

1 Corinthians 1:10

Belonging Together: The Gift of Unity

Read 1 Corinthians 1:4–18.

The body is a unit, though it is made up of many parts; and though all its parts are many, they form one body. So it is with Christ.
1 Corinthians 12:12

"I think we should use a neutral blue for the new carpet in our worship area. Unless we use blue, I won't contribute."

"Blue will never work with our Christmas decorations! I'll fight tooth and nail against the use of blue!"

Ever hear a conversation like the one above? Perhaps the disagreement swirled around ...

- ministry goals;
- using banners (or guitars or liturgy);
- the past vs. present pastor's style; or even
- carpet color!

Because of our sinful, selfish natures we often give offense and take offense—sometimes despite our best intentions. Sometimes these fissures are only tiny tears, but even the

16

tiniest tear has the potential to become a gaping wound in the Body of Christ.

We like to think the early church was exempt from such discord, but nothing could be further from the truth. In fact, most of the New Testament letters read like a correspondence course in conflict resolution! In Corinth, for example, heated arguments and ungodly cliques threatened to rip apart the unity God had given this group of believers. That's why Paul spends a great deal of time in his first letter to this church explaining the importance of unity in the Church.

In the human body many parts work together for the good of the whole. Imagine the havoc if your two feet suddenly headed in opposite directions or your muscles refused to obey your brain's commands. In fact, when accident or illness causes this kind of disruption, doctors and therapists work diligently to bring all the parts back into unity.

Just as two feet walking in opposite directions would incapacitate the body, so disunity in the church makes it harder for the Body of Christ to carry out Christ's work. Outreach. Discipleship. Care. Education. Every ministry suffers when strife and discord rule.

Praise God that in the cross of our Savior he forgives our quarreling and self-focus. And praise him that he works in us what he asks of us—that we "be perfectly united in mind and thought" (1 Corinthians 1:10).

Lord Jesus, unite everyone in our congregation in the love your Holy Spirit creates! Then energize us for . . .

Serving Together: The Gift of Harmony

Read Romans 12:9–21.

Live in harmony with one another.
Romans 12:16

The conductor raises his baton; the audience quiets. The maestro gives the upbeat, and ... Cacophony! Clamor! Racket! Noise! Violins play their own tune, trumpets blast a different melody, and the pianist sits in stunned silence. The members of this orchestra might all be accomplished musicians, but if they aren't playing together, they can't make music. No harmony here!

In Romans 12, Paul compares the smooth interplay of believers' gifts to a symphony and then to the human body. How ridiculous it would be if one's feet or ears would refuse to be part of the body because they don't feel as important as hands and eyes! In the same way, each part of the Body of Christ has an important role to play. No one can legitimately consider his or her gifts "lesser."

Averting our eyes, wringing our hands, and choosing not to use our gifts because they seem insignificant in comparison with the giftedness of others is false humility. As a pastor's wife, I've sometimes had to use my lesser gifts.

18

One Body

My keyboard skills, for example, are barely adequate. But over the years, all that practice has made a difference and—to my amazement my lesser gift has blossomed!

If false humility hurts the church, so does false pride. The eye can't tell the hand, "I don't need you!" Nor can the head sneer at the feet, "You're expendable." So in the church, all of us need to affirm and value everyone else's giftedness and importance.

The part you play is vital! Elder. Dishwasher. Preschool teacher. Lawn mower. Greeter. You are needed! Whether you light the candles, arrange the chairs, or direct the entire Christian education program, you are key. Your congregation could not function as well without you.

What a privilege to be part of the Body of Christ! What an honor to use the gifts he has given for his glory!

Whether you volunteer or serve on the paid staff, your Lord invites and uses the music you make. By his grace, your work makes it possible for your congregation to function like a finely tuned orchestra. Your work matters, even if no one notices the counterpoint you play until that great day when God greets you joyfully, "Well done, good and faithful servant" (Matthew 25:21).

Thank you, Lord, for giving me the privilege of serving you by serving your people! Show me . . .

Working as One: The Gift of Cooperation

Read 1 Corinthians 12:1–6.

There are many parts, but one body.
1 Corinthians 12:20

We've talked about being of one mind in the church, about using whatever gifts God has given us, and about affirming the gifts he has given others. All this is key.

But even if we do all these things, there's still something missing. We will accomplish nothing without cooperation. If unity and harmony are the wheels, cooperation is the oil that makes the whole assembly run smoothly and with minimal friction.

The healthy human body is a miracle of cooperation. Hands fly together over the keys as we type; muscles pull and strain in unison as we heave and lift. Acids in the stomach digest our food, the intestines extract the nutrients from it, and our blood carries the nutrients to every working cell in our body. What a picture of interdependence and cooperation!

Paul uses this picture to emphasize the unity of Christ's Body, the Church. Though this Body has many members,

God intends us to cooperate in such a way that our unity and harmony shine! Each of us works together for the good of all.

In the human body, noncooperative elements can be dangerous. If the stomach refuses to cooperate with the digestive system, we're in for a mighty big stomachache! And we all know what happens when our brain and our hands don't quite engage with one another; a river of spilled milk or a lapful of potato salad most often ensues.

What happens in a church when members don't cooperate? Sometimes individuals walk off the job, intimidated by a do-it-my-way-or-else attitude on the part of others. Sometimes a project heads off in multiple directions, resulting in a hodgepodge result. Sometimes tempers flare and feelings are hurt.

As long as we live in the Church on earth, we will have plenty to forgive in one another! And we will have ample reason to treasure the pardon our Savior earned for us on his own cruel cross.

Trusting God's declaration of forgiveness, we come to center our cooperation not on working *with* others, but on working *for* Christ. In self-sacrificial love, we want the best for our fellow believers, because that's what Christ wants. We aim at achieving his purposes, not our own. In that climate, unity and care flourish.

Lord Jesus, remind me again and again that everything I do is for you! Give me the self-forgetfulness that . . .

Honoring Each Other = The Gift of Respect

Read 1 Corinthians 12:14–26.

The parts that we think are less honorable we treat with special honor. And the parts that are unpresentable are treated with special modesty.
1 Corinthians 12:23

Sit back. Relax. It's been a long, hard day. Slip those aching feet into a tub of warm water. Savor the comfort seeping through your body. Feet might not be beautiful, but they certainly get our respect and, often, the royal treatment!

Feet aren't the only parts of the body that are less than lovely. Most of us seldom consider our internal organs. We never see and rarely think about our spleen or kidneys. We might not even know for sure how these organs function, but we do know one thing—God has placed each member of our body in just the right place for our good.

What do undistinguished body parts have to do with the Church? Plenty! Just as many members of our physical bodies are essential but not usually noticed or noticeable, so too, many essential members of Christ's Body avoid the attention given to other members.

Many of these members prefer to work away from the limelight. They provide the background music in the hum of church activity. Who pays attention to the person who always makes sure there's paper on the roll in the bathroom? No one—until one day that roll is empty. Who notices the gardener who digs out the weeds in the flower beds behind the church building? Who provides public praise for the person who spreads the deicer on the church steps early every frosty Sunday morning?

All these people—and many more like them—make an important difference, as important a difference as those who serve more visibly. And just as we thank God for the toes and lungs that serve our physical bodies without much applause, so too, we honor the quiet, behind-the-scenes members of Jesus' Body.

A simple thank-you note will hearten the kitchen worker who wonders if anyone notices her service. And that elderly man who loves to hand out treats to the Sunday school children? A pat on the back makes him stand just a little straighter.

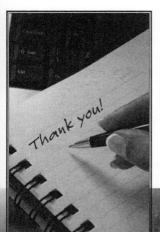

Maybe you serve behind the scenes yourself. Maybe you consider yourself an agent in your congregation's "secret service." If so, good for you! Whether other members notice you or not, your Lord sees. He knows. And he smiles!

Lord, open my eyes and show me someone to thank today! . . .

Caring for Each Other: The Gift of Love

Read 1 Corinthians 12:27–31.

If one part suffers, every part suffers with it; if one part is honored, every part rejoices with it.
1 Corinthians 12:26

My husband served as pastor of a small-town parish in Nebraska for many years. When he developed cancer, he underwent several rounds of chemotherapy, radiation, and surgery. Help appeared from everywhere. Someone cut our grass. Meals appeared seemingly from out of nowhere. The prayer chain sprang to life and continued for months. On the last day of Paul's chemo, balloons and messages of congratulations bedecked our door. What blessings!

While the names and other details may vary, you have probably participated in similar episodes of care and concern. Compassionate care goes along with being part of the Body of Christ.

When one of us suffers, all suffer. Just as one's entire physical body aches when a bone breaks or a head wound needs stitches, so we commiserate when a fellow believer is in pain. We share tough times, illnesses, despair.

We bring a kind word, a casserole, a meaningful Bible verse. Opportunities for service blossom—and as we serve, we blossom, too. We become more and more the kind of people Jesus has created and called us to be.

Just as our Lord entrusts us with the responsibility for sharing hard times with other members of his Body, he gives us the joy of sharing their blessings. When others are honored, Jesus works in us genuine joy at their success. When someone compliments our hair or eyes or athletic abilities, we feel great. Likewise, when other members of the Body of Christ are honored, we can celebrate with them.

We grieve and rejoice with those in our local church. But our compassion extends further. Is your neighbor worrying about his lost dog? Listen and help him! Did a co-worker receive a hoped-for promotion? Share her joy! Who knows? You may even open the door to invite your friend to worship with you. You may have occasion to share Jesus' love in words as well as actions.

As Jesus served, so we serve. In sorrow, we comfort; in times of joy, we rejoice. How privileged we are to bring God's own love and care to those whose lives touch ours!

Lord, teach all of us in your family to rejoice with those who rejoice and weep with those who weep. Especially . . .

For Reflection . . .

Loved unconditionally by our heavenly Father,
we get to reflect his love to others. As God in his
eternal love cherishes and cares for us, we learn
to cherish and care for each other. Unity,
harmony, cooperation, respect, and concern
then follow.

Read Romans 12:4–8; 1 Corinthians 12:27–31;
and Colossians 3:23–24. Then list the gifts God
has given you, both large and small. During the
next week or two, find a way to use each of
those gifts within your congregation. Then jot
down the lessons you learn as you freely share
your gifts.

One Lord

We have different gifts, according to the grace given us. If a man's gift is prophesying, let him use it in proportion to his faith. If it is serving, let him serve; if it is teaching, let him teach; if it is encouraging, let him encourage; if it is contributing to the needs of others, let him give generously; if it is leadership, let him govern diligently; if it is showing mercy, let him do it cheerfully.

Romans 12:6–8

Eyes on the Cross!

Read Romans 12:1–2.

We have different gifts.
Romans 12:6

I don't have the strongest, most effective voice for singing in the choir. Many times I've been tempted to quit. But often someone will stop me after church to say, "The anthem touched my heart. Thank you!" That's when I realize that singing in the choir is not about my voice, but about the Spirit at work.

All those evenings spent going over soprano, alto, tenor, and bass parts and getting all the voices to sing in harmony come together to produce worship-enhancing music in praise of Christ, our Savior.

In a similar way, our gifts, talents, and abilities are most effective when we use them in harmony with the giftedness of others. Everyone's contribution adds to the texture, tone, and richness God intended when he blessed his Church with different gifts.

The possibilities all sound so beautiful, don't they? We long for the reality. But far too often we turn God's good gifts into a reason for disharmony. We compare our gifts to those of others. We envy gifts we deem of higher worth than our own. We resent it when others do not give us the recognition we feel we deserve. Some of us suppose our gifts too small to matter and excuse ourselves from serving. This disharmony—this sin—sours the sweet sound God desires to hear from his people.

In rehearsal, choir directors frequently remind singers to keep "all eyes on me." Similarly, as we serve in Christ's Church, we hear our heavenly Father saying, "Keep all eyes on the cross of my Son!" Looking there, we're embraced by the love of Christ and assured in the forgiveness it offers. Our disharmony melts away as our focus shifts from ourselves to him. Whatever our God-given gifts, each of us is privileged to be among those graced by his calling to work for the strengthening and growth of his Church.

Praise God for the gifts he has given you for carrying out this task. Thank him for the opportunities you have to use your gifts for the good of others. Reflect on ways you can develop your individual talents and abilities even further and on ways you might mentor others within your congregation.

With your eyes on Christ's cross, let your work and the work of others around you rise to the heavens as an anthem of beauty, joy, and harmony!

Lord Jesus, focus my eyes on you and on your cross. Then use me . . .

Burdened and Resentful?

Read 1 Kings 19:1–18.

[Elijah said,] "I have had enough, LORD ..."
1 Kings 19:4

Several names show up repeatedly in our church newsletter's thank-you list. Clearly, these people give generously of their time and abilities, and their example encourages me to participate as fully as possible in the worship and social life of my church family.

Our Lord asks each of us to serve, teach, encourage, and lead—all in proportion to our abilities. Without doubt, he has seen to it that there's something for everyone to do, a role for each to fill, in his Church!

Elijah prophesied. And after awhile, fear and fatigue sapped his abilities. He felt all alone—the only true servant of the Lord in an ocean of unbelief and apathy. He ran away from his responsibilities (literally)! And he wanted to die.

You already serve Jesus by serving the people in his Church. And in doing that, you have learned that it's easy to feel alone, abandoned in your service. You probably aren't in fear for your life as Elijah was. But your burdens may be real, nonetheless. In every age, Satan has a way of turning upside down what God has intended for the good of his people!

30

One Body

Perhaps in your church, like many others, a small, core group of people show up for meetings, program planning, and workdays. When too few people take on too many tasks, zeal often plummets. Stress overshadows joy. It's a recipe for burnout.

If you feel overwhelmed by your service with and among God's people, take some time today to reflect:

- Have you lost sight of God's will for you? If so, how did that happen?
- What resentments might you bring to the cross of your Savior? What reluctance to delegate? What feelings of self-importance?

Then, assured of Christ's forgiveness and under the guidance of his Word and his Spirit, evaluate your service:

- What tasks could you delegate or, at least, find help in doing?
- What might you stop doing? How might you get your schedule back into alignment with the time, energy, and abilities God has entrusted to you?
- Many tasks can be broken down into chunks. How could you do that, providing training to make tasks easier for volunteers to take on?

Father, lead me to delegate in a way that is pleasing to you and that allows those around me to experience the joy of . . .

The Lord Added to Their Number

Read Acts 2:42–47.

If it is contributing to the needs of others, let him give generously.
Romans 12:8

As Paul encouraged believers to exercise and express their various gifts in the Church, he also urged generosity. The apostle, inspired by the Holy Spirit, envisioned vibrant families in which each person would freely contribute the gifts God had given him or her—whether money, property, talents, gifts, or abilities. No matter what needed to be done, a willing servant of God would show up to do it, and do it wholeheartedly.

Yet Paul was no Pollyanna. He knew that God's people, sinners all, often act selfishly. Some of us doubt our abilities. Some of us choose to serve sparingly. Some of us deny our talents and offer nothing. As we look inside ourselves, as we consider our own past behavior, we see ourselves reflected in these descriptions. We see our own weaknesses and reluctance, our uncertainties and limitations.

Our natural tendency is to pull back, deciding that our contribution, or the lack of it, will make little difference. But consider this: When the Holy Spirit descended on the apostles at Pentecost, they shared immediately with anyone who would listen, using the gifts God supplied (Acts 2:1–12). And there were many listeners on that festive day!

Many came to saving faith. And from that point on, enabled and empowered by the Spirit, many gave themselves unreservedly to the work of Jesus Christ, teaching and preaching his message of forgiveness and salvation in Jerusalem and beyond.

The result?

The Lord added to their number daily those who were being saved.
Acts 2:47

God's mode of operation has not changed! Still today, God takes care of our needs for clothing, food, and shelter as we honor him in firstfruits giving. I've found he does the same when I give my time. When my service to his people comes first in my heart, mind and actions, somehow everything else on my schedule falls into place.

It is still by the working of the Holy Spirit that we are able to serve generously, sharing with others our many gifts, talents, and abilities. Energized by Spirit-flamed faith, we strive to use our gifts and also to nurture in others the gifts God has given them, so that his family continues to grow even more vibrant, more dynamic.

Lord, I need you so much! You have given yourself into death for me and you continue to serve me in so many ways. Show me . . .

Many Gifts

Serving by Leading

Read John 13:1–17.

*If it is leadership,
let him govern diligently.*
Romans 12:8

Perhaps you have read or heard about servant leadership. Though popularized in the 1970s by business leader Robert K. Greenleaf, the concept of governing with an attitude of justice, humility, and caring is not new. Early in the history of the Israelites, God laid out his expectations concerning those who would rule over his people. He required each of Israel's kings to copy the Scriptures available then (the five Books of Moses) and to read them daily so that . . .

*. . . his heart may not be lifted up above his brothers,
and that he may not turn aside from the commandment,
either to the right hand or to the left.*
Deuteronomy 17:20 ESV

Whether or not we hold an office, head a committee, teach a class, or direct a group, each of us is a leader in the church. We lead by using our gifts, talents, and abilities with and among others, and by serving in various ways. Other people, especially younger Christians, notice our actions and attitude as we worship and work in God's house. No matter what we are doing, we are leading by example.

As a leader, however, the temptation to "lord it over" our brothers and sisters in Christ will be there. We must fight the temptations to make ourselves more visible and to consider ourselves more important than others.

Our Lord Jesus was well aware of this when he entrusted to us the privilege and responsibility of leadership. For our sins of pride and selfishness, he allowed himself to be lifted up—not to sit on a throne, but to hang on a cross. Our King suffered death for the sake of each of us, his servants. Our Leader accepted the torments of hell itself so that we, his followers, could escape.

In his life, death, and resurrection for us, our Savior demonstrated true, godly leadership. He modeled for us what he wants to work in us. So now, with your eyes on his cross and on his selfless service for you, reflect a bit on your personal leadership attitudes and practices. Let the Holy Spirit shape your heart and help you assume a servant's posture as you take on the leadership tasks before you this week.

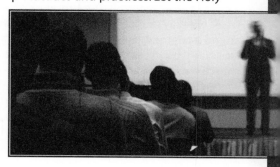

Create in me a clean heart, O God, a servant's heart, as I serve your people by leading . . .

Joy in Serving

Read Colossians 3:15–24.

The one who does acts of mercy,
with cheerfulness.
Romans 12:8 ESV

Christian congregations form when believers come together in Jesus' name for worship, service, learning, and witness. One by one, members join hearts and hands to preach, teach, visit the sick, serve on committees, and sweep the floors. When people pitch in, the church runs smoothly. But it would be a mistake to think of a church in the same ways we think about other organizations. In the church, the tasks we take on are not mere chores to do. Rather, they are privileges to be embraced.

It's easy to forget that. In the busyness of any given day or week, we may find ourselves begrudging the need to attend a committee meeting or visit a shut-in. We may wish we could spend the afternoon at home rather than at the church cleaning the kitchen, folding the newsletters, or wiping the windows. Our resentful attitude can eclipse the motives that led us to sign up in the first place. We forget the truth that we serve our Lord Jesus as we serve his people.

Weak and sinful though we are, our Lord has entrusted to us the work of caring for his people. We do this in all kinds of ways. And as we do, he invites us to move our eyes away from ourselves and back to him and his cross.

One Body

There, we find him reaching out to us, assuring us of his forgiveness. There, we kneel in humility and weakness, receiving from him the strength only his Spirit can provide. There, we receive a new beginning and the attitude of genuine joy only he can give.

With his cross before our eyes, we remember we aren't just doing a job, but receiving a privilege. We don't *have* to do what we do; we *get* to do it!

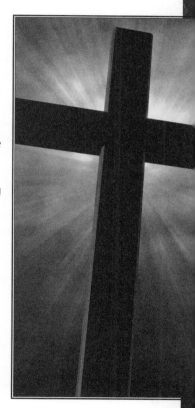

The next time you walk into your church building to serve, take a moment first to enter the sanctuary, the worship area. Imagine yourself standing there, beneath the cross, among all God's saints of every age whose service has made it possible for you to hear and believe the Good News. Then thank him for the joy and privilege of using your gifts for him not as a "got to," but as a "get to"!

Lord, forgive my petty resentments and unthankfulness as I serve. Teach me to thank you for . . .

For Reflection . . .

Read Matthew 5:14–16.

- How are you "letting your light shine" by using your God-given gifts?
- How can you more consistently direct credit to your Savior for the good you are able to do?

Read 1 Corinthians 12:4–6.

- How can you promote recognition and honor for all who serve within your congregation?
- How can you help others develop and use their God-given gifts?

Read John 13:1–17.

- What does Jesus' example of servant leadership mean to you?
- How does his example inform your work and your attitude?

One Church

*Make every effort to keep the
unity of the Spirit through the
bond of peace. There is one
body and one Spirit—
just as you were called to one
hope when you were called—
one Lord, one faith, one
baptism; one God and
Father of all, who is
over all and through
all and in all.*
Ephesians 4:3–6

The One Church

Read Psalm 119:129–135.

The unfolding of your words gives light;
it gives understanding to the simple.
Psalm 119:130

When someone asks about your church membership, you might respond by saying something like this: "We go to *(name)*, that church with the big cross out front."

We usually think in terms of being a member of the church at a specific location. And that's not wrong. But while we're a part of the Body of believers in a specific, *visible* congregation, we're also part of the one holy Christian Church throughout the world—an *invisible* Church, as it were, the one true Church made up of Christians from every nation and tongue. One Church. Christ's Church. The Body of Christ. The Bride of Christ.

Just before his death, Jesus prayed that all his people would be unified: "May [all believers] be brought to complete unity to let the world know that you sent me and have loved them even as you have loved me" (John 17:23).

Complete unity?! Given the many different denominations, worship styles, and doctrinal emphases evident in congregations everywhere, "complete unity" is surely impossible, isn't it? No! In fact, Scripture indicates that in the cross, our Savior's prayer has already been answered.

One Body

Consider the unity you enjoy with other Christ followers throughout the world and down through time. This unity is God's finished, perfect work in Christ. In Ephesians 4:3, Paul urges that we eagerly *maintain* the unity of the Spirit in the bond of peace. We "maintain" what we already have!

God has gathered his believing children into one family in Christ. But there's a big difference between this God-created unity *of* the Church and our day-by-day unity *in* the Church, that unity which we seek to express as we live out our lives in love together as Christ's servants.

You belong to the one Church. You are perfectly united in Christ, covered in the righteousness Jesus won for us in his cross and resurrection. Your faithful service and life of love as God's forgiven child helps maintain that unity of the Spirit in the bond of peace.

We have been won by One and through that One, Jesus Christ, we are one—connected to each other through Christ's love and in service to others!

Thank you for serving the Savior . . . in his one Church!

Lord Jesus, thank you for the unity you create in your Body, the Church. Teach us to honor you always, even when we disagree. Lead me to . . .

The Simple Church

Read John 10:7–18.

*I open my mouth and pant,
longing for your commands.*
Psalm 119:131

Church. The concept seems so simple, doesn't it? The reformer, Martin Luther, wrote that even a seven-year-old child knows what the Church is, namely holy believers, sheep who hear the voice of their Shepherd.

That Shepherd once promised:

*My sheep listen to my voice; I know them,
and they follow me. I give them eternal life, and they shall
never perish; no one can snatch them out of my hand.*
John 10:27–28

The apostle Paul writes:

*There is one body and one Spirit—just as you were called to
one hope when you were called— one Lord, one faith,
one baptism; one God and Father of all,
who is over all and through all and in all.*
Ephesians 4:4–6

Summing this up, we can say that *the* Church—*Christ's* Church—is made up of believers who hear and listen to the voice of their Shepherd-Savior. The Church includes all of

42

One Body

God's people who live eternally by grace through faith in Jesus Christ—the one Savior, Lord over all, through all, and in all.

Maybe, then, I should rephrase my opening question:
Church. It should be so simple, shouldn't it?

In many ways it is simple! But we complicate things by acting in childish, rather than childlike, ways. We want God to listen to our voice and respond to our demands, rather than tuning our ears to listen to his. We walk by sight, not by faith. We prioritize temporary goals, rather than living with an eye toward eternity. And soon we find less joy in serving.

Time and time again I've found myself wallowing in self-pity or overcome by insecurities in ministry. But most of the time those struggles are self-inflicted and unnecessary, brought on by a misdirected focus. My worth and my effectiveness in ministry come only in and through my Jesus, who lives in me.

Thankfully, our Savior has not and cannot abandon his Church. As his Spirit calls, his children come running from every nation, standing together as one at the foot of his cross. There he makes it simple again.

One empty cross. One empty tomb. One Church filled with his grateful, forgiven children who find joy in serving him. It's simple. One Church singing with one voice, "Jesus loves me, this I know!"

Father, forgive me for the sinful attitudes and words in me that have led to disunity and arguments in your family. Teach me to . . .

The Maturing Church

Read Ephesians 4:11–16.

Keep steady my steps according to your promise, and let no iniquity get dominion over me.
Psalm 119:133 ESV

One hot summer night when our children were young, they wanted to read the Christmas story before heading to bed. Not far into the story our then-five-year-old son asked, "How does Jesus get small again every Christmas?" What a great childlike question!

It led my adult mind to consider not so much how, but why he gets small again every Christmas. Could one answer be that our Savior wants to teach us to "get small" again every Christmas—to become like wide-eyed, uninhibited children, as year by year we celebrate the miracle we call Christmas?

We have often heard Christ's call to childlike faith and humility. (See Mark 10:13–16.) But Scripture also reminds us that in all things we are to "grow up into him who is the Head, that is, Christ" (Ephesians 4:15). So what's it going to be? A childlike faith? Or a mature faith? Yes. That's right, both!

We know that human beings can survive without limbs. Every day tragic accidents, war, and disease claim fingers,

44

hands, arms, and even legs from many individuals in our world. It's unimaginably hard, but people do adapt. No one can live, though, without a head! Jesus is the Head of the Church, and he calls us, the members of his Body, to grow into a mature faith while maintaining a childlike trust in him.

The Holy Spirit grows and matures this childlike faith in us, using his Word to nourish us. Connected to the Head, the members of Christ's Body begin to act and live as one. As we mature, love wins! Heaven's wisdom drives our decisions! Hope lives in us! Joy runs with abandonment! Grace fuels compassion and outreach! Scripture's truths conquer! Forgiveness covers hurt! Christ rules!

So, like five-year-old kids at Christmas, let's run to the manger—even if it is August or March! Then it's off to the cross for a lesson in selfless love and the unlimited grace of God. Then we'll race to the garden tomb as the Spirit resurrects our hope. Finally, we'll rest in God's Word, discovering ways the Holy Spirit creates in us a "growing up" faith (rather than a grown-up faith).

And in all this, we will "grow up into him who is the Head, that is, Christ" (Ephesians 4:15).

Jesus, you are the Head of your Church. By your Word, grow me up into more and more childlike faith . . .

The Serving Church

Read Psalm 139.

Redeem me from the oppression of men, that I may obey your precepts.
Psalm 119:134

A bodybuilder friend and I talked today about Psalm 139:13–14:

For you created my inmost being; you knit me together in my mother's womb. I praise you because I am fearfully and wonderfully made; your works are wonderful.

Not surprisingly, my friend could relate to the "body language" in the psalm, and he shared some insights. For instance, he reminded me of our body's intricate and creative design. Our Creator has given each body part a precise purpose, place, and function. He's joined all the parts to all the other parts to create a whole that works with strength, precision, and ease. Our bodies are amazing creations! We don't think about that often enough.

My friend's words made me think of these words from Ephesians 4:16:

From [Christ] the whole body, joined and held together by every supporting ligament, grows and builds itself up in love, as each part does its work.

46

One Body

Here in Ephesians, Paul repeats a word picture he uses in several other letters—the Church as the Body of Christ. Notice, though, what he adds in this verse: the support we give one another helps build the body.

I don't often think about the Church in these terms. But I need to! It would encourage me! In the Body of Christ, we each have a purpose, place, and function. We serve one another and reach out to those who are not, as yet, a part of the Body.

As I talked with my friend, I realized that God has called me to be a bodybuilder too. No, I don't intend to start lifting *weights*; instead, I'll *wait* for his help. You see our Lord is *the* Body Builder. He has built my body and his Body—the Body of Christ, the Church. He has called me to be a part of it, not the only part or the most important part, but a key part. Now, Jesus asks me and all believers to live a body-builder lifestyle. He wants us to build each other up in love as we each carry out the works of service he gives us to do.

Don't you love talking with the Body Builder? Don't you love that he's connected you to himself and to the others in his Body? Don't you love the honor of serving him by serving others?

Lord Jesus, make me a body builder—your Body builder! Teach me to encourage . . .

The Perfect Church?

Read 1 Corinthians 1:1–9.

Streams of tears flow from my eyes,
for your law is not obeyed.
Psalm 119:136

Thank you for serving the Savior in the perfect church!

What? The perfect church?! You may be thinking, "Oh, you don't know *my* church or you wouldn't say that!"

Every week, imperfect people come together in Christian churches to worship a perfect Savior. Every week, forgiven sinners come together in Christian churches to worship a forgiving Savior. Every week, imperfect, forgiven sinners serve the perfect, forgiving Servant, who empowers and encourages the hearts of his servants.

It's easy to focus on the imperfections of people and churches. Satan loves to tempt us with that, using it to create a stumbling block along the path of our faith walk. If you find yourself challenged to serve with joy in an imperfect church right now, ask the Holy Spirit for a reset, a refocus.

A focus on our perfect Savior makes it possible for us to see much more clearly. We realize that his perfection covers his people, and we rejoice in that. As we bask in his forgiveness, grace, and salvation for ourselves, we find strength to serve with purpose, on purpose. The hope-drenched news of Christ crucified and Christ resurrected saturates our thoughts and actions.

Our perfect Savior calls us to grow into more mature, Christlike servants as the Holy Spirit works more faith and deeper love in us. Though imperfect, we find ourselves, by grace, forgiven and connected to Jesus Christ. In his Body, his Church, we discover anew that Jesus is our source of life; he is life itself!

Jesus joins us with other believers. He keeps us connected to him and to one another. As he builds us up in his perfect love, we respond, in turn, by building up each other in his love.

So, in a sense, we do serve in a perfect church, but only because his perfection covers his Body. While we're imperfect sinners, we are also holy saints because Christ died—and rose—for us.

And one day when Christ returns, he'll gather all of his faithful believers in perfect unity to spend eternity with him in the perfection of heaven. For all eternity our joy will be complete as we serve the One, who came to serve and save.

Lord, I am far from perfect and my church is far from perfect. But you cover our imperfections. Grant . . .

For Reflection . . .

Spend some quiet time with Jesus, alone.
Schedule it in your calendar. Ask yourself:

• How would someone with a childlike faith
respond to Christ's presence? How do I?
What will I say to him about that?

• In what ways am I maturing in faith while
not leaving childlike trust behind? What will
I ask Jesus to do for me in both maturity
and childlikeness?

Consider singing or humming "Jesus Loves Me,
This I Know." Imagine your Savior leading you
along the path to his empty cross and tomb.
Respond as the Holy Spirit moves you.

One Savior

*I thank my God every time
I remember you.
In all my prayers for all of you,
I always pray with joy because
of your partnership in the
gospel from the first day until
now, being confident of this,
that he who began a good
work in you will carry it on
to completion until the day
of Christ Jesus.*
Philippians 1:3–6

You're Welcome!

Read Philippians 1:3–6.

I thank my God every time I remember you. In all my prayers for all of you, I always pray with joy.
Philippians 1:3–4

Thankful words encourage. That being said, I'd like to thank you for serving the Savior! You use your giftedness to serve and honor our Savior within the one Body of Christ. Thank you for doing that!

Thank you. Those two little words hold a lot of power. Consider the way simple words of gratitude can impact your moments and days. When someone says, "Thank you!" you automatically respond, "You're welcome!" (Your mother and father would be so proud!)

But our heavenly Father's ways are different from the ways of the world. In fact, they're reversed! Think about it. You have a saving faith not because of something you did or said, but because your Savior said, "You're welcome— welcome to the family of God!"

You serve because Jesus, the Master Servant, first said, "You're welcome—welcome to a world of humble service. Follow my lead!"

Your certainty of complete forgiveness, abundant life, and eternal salvation has come to you because your Savior flung wide his arms of grace on the cross and said, "You're welcome—welcome to my kingdom for eternity!"

The world's Savior, Jesus Christ, welcomes us into a world of grace, of undeserved love. He welcomes us into a life overflowing with gifts like hope, joy, peace, constant companionship, and undying love.

Now you can celebrate the day the Holy Spirit came to you, creating faith within you and welcoming you into the kingdom of God. You can rejoice each day upon awakening as you hear your Savior say, "My child, you're welcome to enjoy my grace in the space in which I have placed you!" Hearing the welcoming words of your Savior, you can respond in humility, joy, and faith: "Thank you!"

Jesus once told his disciples, "You did not choose me, but I chose you and appointed you to go and bear fruit—fruit that will last" (John 15:16). Once again today, Jesus reminds you that he has chosen you for the joy of serving him. His choice does not depend on anything you have done or will do.

Instead, he says to you, "You're welcome! Welcome to the kingdom of God! Welcome to the freedom and life I have won for you through my life, death, and resurrection!"

You're welcome!

Thank you, Jesus, for your welcome! It has changed my life! Show me how to serve you today . . .

Remember . . .
with
Thanksgiving

Read Psalm 78.

They remembered that God was
their Rock, that God Most High
was their Redeemer.
Psalm 78:35

Both good and bad memories fill our minds, especially
since memories are all we really know. This present
moment becomes a memory as soon as . . . there it goes! It's
a memory already!

Many of the Bible's "remember" passages remind us that
God faithfully remembers his promises.

[God said,] "I will remember my covenant between me and you
and all living creatures of every kind. Never again will the
waters become a flood to destroy all life."
Genesis 9:15

In other passages, God's people plead with him to
remember his faithful promises:

Remember, O LORD, your great mercy and love,
for they are from of old.
Psalm 25:6

Sometimes, but not nearly often enough, God's people remember him:

> They remembered that God was their Rock,
> that God Most High was their Redeemer.
> Psalm 78:35

At other times, God asks his people to remember his promises as they come together in faith. For example, when Jesus instituted the Lord's Supper, he asked that we eat and drink this Meal in remembrance of him (1 Corinthians 11:23–25).

While all of us would rather forget the times we've disobeyed and disappointed our Lord, what a blessing to remember our Savior took all our sins upon himself, giving us in return forgiveness and hope for the future! Jesus forgives each of us, and he brings all of his people into relationship with one another in his Church. He joins us together with other believers and makes us one—one Savior and one Body, with many members. Like the apostle Paul, we gratefully remember those around us who join us in serving our Savior. Paul wrote to his friends in the city of Philippi, "I thank my God every time I remember you" (Philippians 1:3).

God remembers his promises and is faithful to them. He loves to comfort us all when we call out to him, asking that he remember those promises, too. Our Savior gave his life so we could live. And now we get to serve him alongside many others who love him. Remember that today … with thanksgiving!

Lord Jesus, you always remember me—in compassion and love. Remind me to remember you and those who serve you alongside me, especially . . .

Partnership in the Gospel

Read John 15:1–8.

I always pray with joy because of your partnership in the gospel.
Philippians 1:4–5

Partners. They're part of our lives. We find ourselves in business partnerships, marriage partnerships, temporary partnerships formed to complete projects or reach goals, and partnerships in a wider sense through a common group or organization.

Partnerships can challenge, but they can also bring a multitude of blessings! Paul's words to the believers in Philippi emphasize these blessings. The "partnership in the Gospel" Paul so treasures begins with Christ. He has brought us into a relationship with himself and with one another. Jesus describes this connection this way:

I am the vine; you are the branches.
If a man remains in me and I in him, he will bear much fruit;
apart from me you can do nothing.
John 15:5

Our connection with Christ is of supreme importance. All other godly partnerships stem from that one, eternal and essential partnership.

Connected with Christ, we are now connected with others in his Body. It's a unique and powerful partnership. We're so closely connected that when "one part suffers, every part suffers with it; if one part is honored, every part rejoices with it" (1 Corinthians 12:26). We pray for one another, draw strength from the giftedness of others, and encourage each other in this partnership.

It's a joy and privilege to do that! As you pray *for* others, look for opportunities to pray *with* others, too. I have found great blessings and closer connections growing when, instead of telling someone, "I'll pray for you," I have stopped and said, "Would you mind if we prayed about that right now?" Then, together, we brought the concerns to the Lord.

The apostle Paul partnered with individuals and congregations to help people know Christ and make Christ known—a partnership in the Gospel. What a great thought! What a great way to live!

Invited by Jesus into a mission partnership and empowered by him to live it out, we partner with many others to share his love. Yes, we're all sinners, and that makes it difficult at times. But we serve, trusting that our Savior's perfect life covers our imperfections. Forgiven, we extend forgiveness to our brothers and sisters—our partners in mission—too.

Lord Jesus, you bless us with partners in the Gospel. Thank you! Now and forever be the focus of those relationships! Teach me especially to . . .

Gratitude

Read Colossians 1:3–14.

We have not stopped praying for you and asking God to fill you with the knowledge of his will through all spiritual wisdom and understanding.
Colossians 1:9

A previous message in this book emphasized this truth: gratitude encourages. The words *thank you* are empowering and powerful. When others share their gratitude with us, it impacts our moments and days in positive ways.

Perhaps surprisingly, though, when we share our thankfulness with others, it shines the light of Christ's joy into the dimly lit corners of our own lives! There's great blessing in both receiving and giving gifts of gratitude.

When you stop to consider it, our Lord has given us much for which to be thankful. When we home in on specific gifts, we discover more and more blessings. I once created a list with 365 items for which I'm thankful—one for every day of the year. (When I completed it, I discovered I had listed chocolate 12 times!) When I add names of people who partner with me in sharing the Gospel, I easily have another 365 reasons to give thanks—two years of reasons to thank God for his blessings.

As we consider all our blessings—especially the people whose lives bless ours—our thankfulness begins to multiply. It spills over into many expressions of thanksgiving for and to those around us.

That kind of gratitude can open doors for witness. Those who receive your thankful words and see your Christlike example may wonder about it and ask. Then you can share! Jesus urges us:

> Let your light shine before men, that they may see your good deeds and praise your Father in heaven.
> Matthew 5:16

Praying for one another's needs is part of everyday life in Christ's Body, the Church. Usually we do this during times of difficulty or at points in the lives of others when they need discernment and wisdom. But we can also pray with thanksgiving for our brothers and sisters in the faith. And we can let them know about those prayers. Imagine the blessings that might grow from that!

Let these words of Scripture shape your thoughts today and stir up gratitude in your heart:

> Every time you cross my mind, I break out in exclamations of thanks to God. Each exclamation is a trigger to prayer. I find myself praying for you with a glad heart.
> Philippians 1:3–4 The Message

Thank you, life-giving Savior! You've done so much for me! Teach me to express my thankfulness to others . . .

A Full Heart

Read Philippians 1:3–11.

I hold you in my heart, for you are all partakers with me of grace, both in my imprisonment and in the defense and confirmation of the gospel.
Philippians 1:7 ESV

Imagine the apostle Paul writing a line of greeting cards. In my mind's eye, I picture a card covered with hearts. The words on the outside read: *I love you and thank God for you.*

The words inside read: *It is right for me to feel this way about all of you, since I have you in my heart.*

Would a card like that sell? Actually, we might argue that it's already been a best seller for centuries, since these words from Paul's pen appear in the world's best seller of all time—the Holy Bible! Paul shares those words of love in his letter to his Christ-saved friends in Philippi.

As we step into this letter, we read wonderful, welcoming words. Paul's heart overflows with a passion for Jesus and a passion for Jesus' mission. In addition, Paul expresses a passionate commitment to all who serve the Savior in the Body of Christ.

In fact, Paul's passion for Christ and for sharing Christ's message had landed Paul in prison. There, surprisingly, Paul writes a letter of love and deep joy.

Paul's love isn't your everyday kind of love. Paul loves the Philippians "with the affection of Christ Jesus." Paul holds his fellow servants in his heart with the love of Christ. That's the way to love! That's the way to serve the Savior and his people!

Only the Holy Spirit can stir up that kind of passionate, Christlike affection within our hearts. And he wants to do it! He creates it in us through the power of his Word. As we come to understand the forgiving love Jesus freely lavishes on us, we find ourselves loving people we once considered unlovable. We find ourselves forgiving what some deem unforgivable. We see our attitudes and words instilling hope in the hopeless.

Christ's servants, we serve with love and love to serve with joy. A passion for compassion flows from our hearts. All because Jesus lives in us.

Ours is a love fired by the urgency to share the news that has changed our own lives forever—the news of Jesus Christ, of his cross and empty tomb, the news of the One who brings true and eternal life to all who believe in him.

Lord Jesus, you hold me in your heart. You will always love me! Thank you! Now teach me to love . . .

For Reflection ...

- We have so many reasons to give thanks! For which specific blessings would you like to thank your Savior right now?

- How might you show your thankfulness for others within the Body of Christ?

- Consider the ways gratitude has affected you in the last 24 hours. Who has shared their thanksgiving for you with you? Whom have you thanked?

- Pray for a heart overflowing with love and gratitude for your Savior and all he brings into your life each day. Ask that he make you more aware of opportunities to share your gratitude with other people.

Thank You for Serving the Savior!

It's hard to fathom: Jesus' love for you will never end. Never! Who can comprehend a love like that or grasp its magnitude?

Still, despite our incomplete comprehension of our Savior's selfless love on Calvary's cross, we love. We serve as he served. He encourages, and we are encouraged, while encouraging others. Until he returns, we do all this imperfectly, but we do it covered with his own perfection.

And we do it together; we do it in his Body, the Church. One Body. One Lord. One Church. One Savior.

Thank you for serving the Savior!

Thank You for Serving the Savior!

If this book has made a difference in your life or if you have simply enjoyed it, we would like to hear from you. Your words will encourage us! If you have suggestions for us to consider as we create books like this in the future, please send those, too.

Send e-mail to editor@CTAinc.com and include the subject line: TSS1SC.

Write to
Editorial Manager, Department TSS1SC, CTA, Inc.
PO Box 1205, Fenton, MO 63026-1205

Or leave a comment at share.CTAinc.com